TESSA LORANT

Knitted

Lace

Edgings

THE THORN PRESS

Two ways of using lace edgings:

Above, the Marguerite Border used
to display spring flowers

On the right, Machine Edith Lace
used to embellish home-made jam

ONTENTS

Two ways of dressing laces on
solid forms so that the laces
may then be displayed to the
best advantage

INTRODUCTION

Lace knitting is often considered to be difficult. Many people, thinking that only very skilled knitters are able to produce knitted lace, give up without even trying out the craft. This attitude has had several repercussions: the tools of hand lace knitting – traditionally fine steel knitting needles or 'wires' – are no longer made, very few old lace patterns remain in print, even fewer modern lace patterns are available, and the fine yarns needed for lace knitting are hard to find in the High Street.

TOOLS

The finest knitting needles available at the moment are the 1.75 mm (15) and the 1.50 mm (16) sizes, marketed by Aero but not always stocked. These two sizes are valuable for making reasonably fine laces and can be bought in knitting pin pairs of 25, 30 and 35 cm lengths, and in sets of four knitting needles in 20 and 30 cm lengths. Steel needles, in sizes from 1.50 mm (16) upwards and in 16 inch lengths, are available direct from Scotland, and are useful for knitting Shetland lace shawls, and the larger tablecloths or other lace articles.

The finest twin pins or circular needles available are in the 2 mm (14) size, and are particularly helpful for large articles knitted in the round, though it will be necessary to start or finish with a set of needles.

The craft of machine knitting is becoming more and more popular, and a breakthrough in 'transfer' lace knitting has recently been achieved by the introduction of the 'one-action' lace carriage. Though lace carriages have been used to transfer stitches from one needle to an adjacent needle for some time now, the new carriage can select, transfer and knit a row in a single pass of the carriage. It can also be used to select and transfer only, so that the lace hole can be separated from the doubled stitch; but this type of lace knitting will need several moves of the carriage as well as several other adjustments to knit a single row. Machines which have this new facility are no more difficult to work with than ordinary punchcard or electronic machines; so, in effect, automatic transfer lace knitting is now available for some types of knitted lace patterns. This is bound to result in a growing interest in this branch of knitting, and the last 8 edgings in this book are some of the first published machine patterns which transpose traditional hand knitted lace edgings to the 24-space punchcard.

YARNS

Though the very finest crochet yarns are now no longer sold by manufacturers based in this country, fine French yarns are available for the ambitious lace knitter. Apart from these, many of the machine sewing and embroidery threads, fine 'industrial' synthetic yarns, glitter threads and very fine wools also make excellent lace knitting yarns, as do linen and silk threads sold primarily for weaving or pillow lace making. There is, then, no lack of material for the would-be fine lace knitter.

Several firms have recently introduced a large variety of medium weight cotton yarns in 'fancy' forms which are particularly well suited to lace knitting, and even more firms are also spinning unusual yarns in various fibres or fibre mixtures. A short list of manufacturers is given at the end of this book, but much more information about yarns in general as well as a list of specialist suppliers is given in my YARNS FOR THE KNITTER (Thorn, 1980).

PATTERNS

The first 19 patterns in this collection of knitted lace edgings all originally derive from the end of the famous 'white knitting' era of some 100 years ago. These edgings are all made on 2 needles, often on a very small number of stitches, with a set of pattern rows repeated until the required length is knitted. This way of knitting is particularly suitable for the beginner in lace knitting, as it is not too demanding. The patterns have been carefully chosen to represent all kinds of knitted lace, and may well be of interest even to the specialist. None of them is too difficult for the average knitter, and they are illustrated in their eventual 'proper' shape. Some are also shown with an enlarged portion to demonstrate how the individual stitches are made.

These patterns were, of course, all designed for hand knitting. But there is no reason why the knitting machine should not be used to make lace edgings, and I have freely transposed some of the old patterns to the 24-space punchcard for use with the one-action lace carriage supplied with the Knitmaster 260 and 360 machines. These laces will not be the same as the old patterns, because the knitting techniques vary, if only slightly, but they are based on some of the traditional hand knitted laces and their names are borrowed from the original patterns. The patterns are presented as machine knitting patterns in their own right, part of the creative craft of machine knitting. They are meant to be enjoyed by the modern knitter, who often combines hand and machine knitting. They may also encourage them to invent some patterns of their own.

This is not a knitting manual; my HAND AND MACHINE KNITTED LACES (Batsford, 1982) gives detailed directions for both hand and machine knitting techniques. However, it is helpful to very briefly describe the most common techniques used in this book, and this is done beside the symbols shown on pages 12 and 13.

CHARTS

The charts used in this book have been specially invented to replace the usual written pattern form, which is not as convenient. Pattern charts have gone out of favour in this country, though they were once used as much here as anywhere else. They have many advantages, and are given in addition to the usual written instructions. However, the facsimile on page 20, taken from an old knitting book, shows how hard these instructions can be to follow, and how often mistakes occur in printing them. The mistake in this one defeated a number of knitters, and it was not until I charted the design that it became quite clear where the mistake was. Errors in typesetting are quite common in ordinary text, and, when highly technical, repetitive terms are used, such errors are very difficult to avoid. A chart can help to pinpoint them, even if there are errors in the chart itself.

Charts do present a difficulty in flat knitting and this is, perhaps, the reason why they have almost disappeared from modern knitting books written in English. I have written these charts for the hand knitter who uses two needles only; the charts are always read from right to left on the odd rows and from left to right on the even rows, and you knit precisely what you see on the chart.

I have adopted the old method of representing knit stitches on a white ground and purl stitches on a black ground, so that it is immediately obvious whether you are knitting plain or purl. Most of these edgings are knitted on a garter ground, so that most of the stitches will be plain, that is on a white ground. Jersey will show as white and black rows alternating.

SYMBOLS

I have used symbols, or symbols overlapped, found on many modern typewriters so that you can type up your own charts. If you do not have the reversing out facility to make the purl symbols, you can always underline these characters and build up your charts in that way.

Occasionally an asterisk denotes an empty space; this is to help you 'see' the outline of the lace holes properly. The charts give quite a good indication of the outline of the lace edging, though they cannot replace the illustrations. Charts are also very helpful when transposing hand knitting patterns to machine design cards.

DRESSING THE LACES

Knitted lace edgings are not just knitted lace in the usual sense of a textured fabric with lace 'holes' in geometric or figurative patterns; they are rather more than that. Many of the edgings are 'shaped' as well — not merely by using the side shaping so common in ordinary flat knitting, but by using bias and shaping techniques within the fabric. The edgings are carefully constructed to lie on a three-dimensional form, such as the body. They are meant for wearing round the neck, the wrist, the waist, the head and so on. Ordinary flat knitting is not usually contoured in this way. It is, I suspect, the final preparation of the knitted fabric strips which is no longer correctly done. Drying the edgings on a flat surface will not give the correct shape nor show off the lace pattern properly, and ironing them may make it even worse. Pillow laces, after all, are constructed on a pillow so that the lace is, in effect, a curved surface. Unless knitted lace edgings are properly prepared they look a mess – hanging limply from a garment hem, or crumpled round the neck. What they need is body. They need to be starched and then shaped, but before you do this sew the cast on and cast off edges together, in contrasting thread if you want to undo the seam later.

Any method of starching will do to give body to the lace edgings – traditional, instant or spray – and any kind of starch. One of my favourites is sugar: ordinary white household sugar. Dissolve it in cold water for the best effect. The amount you will need depends on the material to be starched. Crochet cottons need a fair amount, say 4 tablespoons in a cup of water; synthetics need only a teaspoon in the same amount of water. The sugar can change the colour of your yarn very slightly, but it will not feel sticky once dry.

Dip your edging into your favourite starch, or simply wet it. You are now in a position to shape your lace without any need to outline the shape on paper or to use pins or anything com-plicated. All you need is a good surface to put them on. Then you can mould them into the shape you like.

The illustration on page 24 will show you better than any number of words one way of shaping a particular lace. Another method is to use a single upturned pudding bowl which will be effective for a whole range of different edging shapes and lengths. All you need do is place the wet lace over your chosen surface and smooth the edging into shape. Make sure that each lace hole is properly displayed, each picot shown off, each serrated or other edge arranged to the best advantage. It helps to use a knitting needle or a blunt-ended tapestry needle to bring out some of the more intricate bits. You need not worry about the curve; that will be formed automatically by the curved form you use. When you are satisfied, just let the laces dry; no geometric guidelines, no pins, no pressing, no ironing. Your lace will be perfectly displayed, the texture will stay intact and it will fit well. Very long edgings will need some thought to dress them satisfactorily; spiralling round a reasonably large form is one solution, but each case needs to be considered separately.

If you attach a deeply curved edging to a straight piece of fabric, it will automatically form a frill, as shown on page 21. As you can see from the copyright page, if you wish to make a crown, you can...

Some of the photographs have been specially treated to make them reminiscent of the period; this also helps one to see precisely how the stitches have been made.

STORING LACE

The illustration on page 23 shows a good way to store lace collars and cuffs, or detachable edgings; the cone overcomes the difficulty of storing the shaped pieces. Straight laces can be wound over cardboard cylinders and then stored in this way.

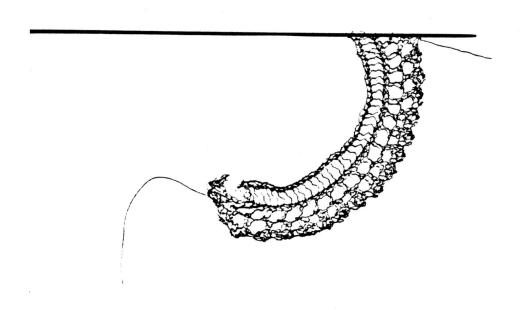

HAND KNITTED LACES

Hand knitted laces are easy to make, cheap to produce, quick to finish and simple to dress and store. I hope you'll try the patterns and see what beautiful additions you can make for your clothes and household linens – real lace at a fraction of the cost of buying, at a fraction of the time needed to make 'bobbin' laces. Some of the patterns, such as Spider Edging and Antique Edging, don't even look like knitting.

If you find you really enjoy the edgings, try your hand at designing your own. Once you've worked your way through the patterns given here, you'll find you can change them a little here and there to make your own individual laces. The charts give you the opportunity to produce quite new ones; it isn't really difficult, once you've got the basic knowledge, and you will acquire that by working your way through the ones in this book.

CASTING OFF

The method of counting the cast off stitches can seem confusing at first. The chart always gives a knit or knitwise slip stitch before the casting off symbols, because you end up with a stitch on the right hand needle after you have cast off the number given. In other words, if the pattern says cast off 3, knit or slip the first stitch, then knit the next to cast off 1, knit another to cast off 2, knit another to cast off 3. You are left with a stitch on the right hand needle. Some patterns look better with the first stitch slipped, others look better when it's knitted. I have used both methods for the illustration of the Epsom Border on page 10; as you can see, it looks much better when the first stitch is slipped.

ACKNOWLEDGMENT

I would like to thank Mrs Queen Hitchcock for her generous help with knitting some of the hand knitted edgings illustrated in this book.

SYMBOLS AND
ABBREVIATIONS

| = K
   knit

‖ = P
   purl

– = Sk
   slip one stitch knitwise

▬ = Sp
   slip one stitch purlwise

0 = 0 (one over)
   Yarn over (round) needle without making a stitch

T = T (one throw)
   Yarn over (thrown round) needle while making a stitch

c = c
   cast on

C = C
   cast off

/ = K2tog
   knit two loops together as though knitting one stitch

+ = SKtog
   slip one knitwise, knit one, pass slipped stitch over

Ⲭ = K3tog
   knit three loops together as though knitting one stitch

⧶ = SK2tog
   slip one knitwise, knit two together, pass slipped
   stitch over

‡ = SSKtog
        slip 2 stitches knitwise to RHN, knit the next
        stitch, then pass the 2 slipped stitches over

* = a space
        this is sometimes put in to make the shape clearer

X = X
        special instructions

If a number follows a symbol or a set of abbreviations in
brackets, the action is repeated that number of times

||6||| =   K6
            knit six stitches

B = border
st = stitch
RHN = right hand needle
LHN = left hand needle

There are many other lace knitting techniques, but they do
not occur in the patterns in this book; any special technique
used is explained in the pattern itself.

C H A R T S

Read the charts from the bottom to the top
Read odd rows from right to left
Read even rows from left to right
Black on a white background represents knit stitches and
techniques
White on a black background represents purl stitches
and techniques

$\mathcal{L}$OOP $\mathcal{E}$DGING

```
0∦|0/|    4
|||/0||    3
|▮|0/|    2
/00/0||    1
```

Cast on 6 stitches and knit 1 row

Row 1:   K2, 0, K2tog, 02, K2tog
Row 2:   K2, P1, K1, 0, K2tog, K1
Row 3:   K2, 0, K2tog, K3
Row 4:   0, SSKtog, K1, 0, K2tog, K1

Repeat rows 1 to 4

This very simple little pattern can be used to make an
edging for curved or rectangular pieces of fabric; the
two illustrations show the same piece of lace shaped as
needed. Remember that the double over needs both a knit
and a purl stitch knitted into it on the return row.
Knitted here in Coats chain mercer crochet 10 on 2.5 mm
(12) needles.

ℬUTTERCUP ℰDGING

```
|C4CC|||0/|   6
||6|||/0||▰    5
||▮||▮||0/|   4
/00/00/0||▰   3
||▮||▮||0/|   2
||00/0||▰     1
```

Cast on 7 stitches and knit 1 row

Row 1:   Sp, K2, O, K2tog, O2, K2
Row 2:   K3, P1, K2, O, K2tog, K1
Row 3:   Sp, K2, O, K2tog, O2, K2tog, O2, K2tog
Row 4:   K2, P1, K2, P1, K2, O, K2tog, K1
Row 5:   Sp, K2, O, K2tog, K6
Row 6:   C4, K3, O, K2tog, K1

Repeat rows 1 to 6

This dainty edging is a little more ambitious, but still
well within the scope of a beginner. It tends to shape
itself into a shallow curve, and is shown here made in
Coats chain mercer crochet 40, knitted on 2 mm (14)
needles.

ℰᴘꜱᴏᴍ ℬᴏʀᴅᴇʀ

```
-CCC|||8|||||0/|        4
||||10|||||/0||▪        3
▪|4|▐▌|▐▌||0/|        2
|4||00/00|/0||▪        1
```

Cast on 12 stitches and knit 1 row

Row 1: Sp, K2, O, K2tog, K1, O2, K2tog, O2, K4
Row 2: Sp, K4, P1, K2, P1, K3, O, K2tog, K1
Row 3: Sp, K2, O, K2tog, K10
Row 4: C3, K8, O, K2tog, K1

Repeat rows 1 to 4

This attractive little lace is shown here worked in Coats chain mercer crochet 40 on 2 mm (14) needles. It is shown on page 10 still on 1 mm (18) needles and worked in the finest crochet yarn available, DMC cordonnet special 120.

The first few row repeats on the left hand side of the very fine lace were finished by knitting the first stitch before casting off 3 stitches; the rest were made by slipping that first stitch, giving a much better definition to the edge.

ℱLORENTINE ℰDGING

```
|CCC|||8|||||█|||    4
/0/0/0/0/0/00||█     3
0||||10|||||█|||     2
/0/0/0/0/00||█       1
```

Cast on 13 stitches and knit 1 row

Row 1: Sp, K2, 02, (K2tog,0)4, K2tog
Row 2: 0, K10, P1, K3
Row 3: Sp, K2, 02, (K2tog,0)5, K2tog
Row 4: C3, K8, P1, K3

Repeat rows 1 to 4

This very easily worked edging twists round into an unex-
pected shape after only two or three pattern repeats; you
will notice that the lace is quite curved even before you
dress it.   After starching and dressing the lace will form
a deep curve.   Knitted here in Moelnlycke crochet cotton
Nm 8 (roughly equivalent to an English 20) on 2.5 mm (12)
needles.

𝓕RISBY 𝓔DGING

```
|CC4C|||||11||||0/|   4
|||||||14||||||/0||▬   3
||▮▮|||▮▮||▮▮||||0/|   2
||/00/00/00/00||0||▬   1
```

Cast on 15 stitches and knit 1 row

Row 1:   Sp, K2, 0, K2tog, K1, (02, K2tog)4, K1
Row 2:   K3, P1, (K2,P1)3, K3, 0, K2tog, K1
Row 3:   Sp, K2, 0, K2tog, K14
Row 4:   C4, K11, 0, K2tog, K1

Repeat rows 1 to 4

Another very simple edging, quite different from the
Florentine in looks but just as easily made, can be used
for dainty collars and cuffs as it will, like the previous
edging, easily form a deep curve.

Both fabric sides are shown, one knitted on size 1.5 mm (16)
needles in Coats chain mercer crochet 60, the other knitted
on size 2 mm (14) needles in Coats mercer crochet size 40.

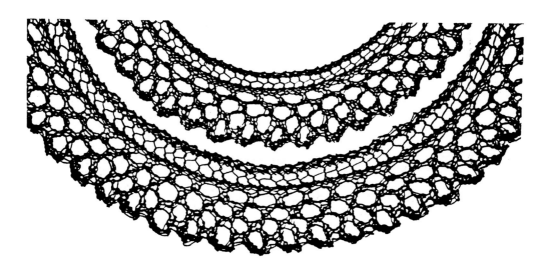

$\mathcal{S}$PIDER $\mathcal{E}$DGING

```
| | | 0 | 0 / 0 | 4 | | 0 / |    6
| | | 0 / | | / 0 | | / 0 | | |    5
| C4CC | 0 / | | | | / 0 | | 0 / |    4
| | 6 | | | 0 | | 5 | | 0 / / 0 | | |    3
| | 6 | | | 0 | | | 0 / | | | 0 / |    2
| | 6 | | | 0 | 0 | | | / 0 | | |    1
```

Cast on 15 stitches and knit 1 row

Row 1: K3, O, K2tog, K3, O, K1, O, K6
Row 2: K6, O, K3, O, K2tog, K3, O, K2tog, K1
Row 3: K3, O, (K2tog)2, O, K5, O, K6
Row 4: C4, K1, O, K2tog, K3, K2tog, O, K2tog, K1, O,
   K2tog, K1
Row 5: K3, O, K2tog, K1, O, K2tog, K1, K2tog, O, K3
Row 6: K3, O, K1, O, SK2tog, O, K4, O, K2tog, K1

Repeat rows 1 to 6

Though this is a simple six row edging, the lace is
quite sophisticated and not very reminiscent of most
knitted laces.   This is a true knitted lace, with
single yarn strands outlining a definite spider body!
Knitted in Coats chain mercer crochet 60 on 1 mm (18)
needles.   An enlarged version of the pattern is shown on
page 41.

DEWDROP EDGING

```
|CC5CC00/00/|▐█▌||0/|   8
||||11|||||0//0||▬      7
||▐█▌|▐█▌|▐4█▌||0/|     6
|/00/00/00|0//0||▬      5
|||8|||▐█▌||0/|         4
▐█▌|▐█▌||0//0||▬        3
|00/00/|▐█▌||0/|        2
||6|||0//0||▬           1
```

Cast on 13 stitches and knit 1 row

Row 1: Sp, K2, 0, (K2tog)2, 0, K6
Row 2: K1, 02, K2tog, 02, K2tog, K1, P2, K2, 0, K2tog, K1
Row 3: Sp, K2, 0, (K2tog)2, 0, K3, P1, K2, P1, K1
Row 4: K8, P2, K2, 0, K2tog, K1
Row 5: Sp, K2, 0, (K2tog)2, 0, K1, (02, K2tog)3, K1
Row 6: K3, P1, K2, P1, K2, P4, K2, 0, K2tog, K1
Row 7: Sp, K2, 0, (K2tog)2, 0, K11
Row 8: C5, (02,K2tog)2, K1, P2, K2, 0, K2tog, K1

Knit rows 1 to 8
Repeat rows 3 to 8; the first 2 rows are foundation rows

No. 25.—DEWDROP EDGING.

CAST on 13 stitches. Knit 1 plain row **1st row**—Slip 1, knit 2, make 1, knit 2 together, knit 2 together, make 1, knit 6. **2nd row**—Knit 1, make 2, knit 2 together, make 2, knit 2 together, knit 1, purl 2, knit 2, make 1, knit 2 together. knit 1. **3rd row**—Slip 1, knit 2 make 1, krit 2 together, knit 2 together, make 1, knit 3, purl 1, knit 2, purl 1, knit 1. **4th row**—Knit 8, purl 2, knit 2, make 1, knit 2 together, knit 1. **5th row**—Slip 1, knit 2, make 1, knit 2 together, knit 2 together, make 1, knit 1, make 2, knit 2 together, make 2, knit 2 together, knit 1. **6th row**—Knit 3, purl 1, knit 2, purl 1, knit 2, purl 4, make 1, knit 2 together, knit 1. **7th row**—Slip 1, knit 2, make 1, knit 2 together, make 1, knit 11. **8th row**—Cast off 5, make 2, knit 2 together, make 2, knit 2 together, knit 1, purl 2, knit 2, make 1, knit 2 together, knit 1. Repeat from the third row.

———

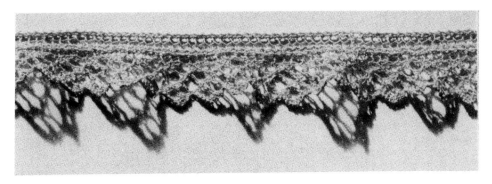

Though knitted in fairly thick yarn, a 20s crochet cotton,
and on relatively thick 2 mm (14) needles, this edging is
still very light and airy. The strong bias gives the lace
a deeply curved edge, and the double overs ensure really
large lace holes. If you straighten the inside curve you
automatically ruffle the edging, as shown in the photo.

The facsimile instructions are faulty; you will see from
the chart what was wrong, and how easily it was put right
by first putting the pattern in chart form. Without the
chart it can be quite difficult to find the mistake, though
the stitch count tells you that it occurs in row 6.

℘RIMROSE ℰDGING

```
|CC6CCC███6███|0/|   8
|||7|||/|0≠0/0||█    7
███|███|███8██|0/|   6
/00/00/|0||0/0||█    5
███|████7███|0/|     4
|/00/|0||0/0||█      3
███|███6██|0/|       2
/00/|0|0/0||█        1
```

Cast on 11 stitches and purl 1 row

Row 1: Sp, K2, 0, K2tog, 0, K1, 0, K1, K2tog, 02, K2tog
Row 2: P2, K1, P6, K1, 0, K2tog, K1
Row 3: Sp, K2, 0, K2tog, 0, K2, 0, K1, K2tog, 02, K2tog, K1
Row 4: P3, K1, P7, K1, 0, K2tog, K1
Row 5: Sp, K2, 0, K2tog, 0, K3, 0, K1, (K2tog, 02)2, K2tog
Row 6: (P2, K1)2, P8, K1, 0, K2tog, K1
Row 7: Sp, K2, 0, K2tog, 0, SK2tog, 0, K1, K2tog, K7
Row 8: C6, P6, K1, 0, K2tog, K1

Repeat rows 1 to 8

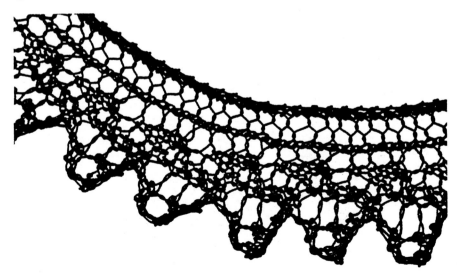

You will see how this edging has been used to form the
letters L and E on the front cover; this gives some
idea of its versatility.   The enlargement on page 22
shows precisely how the stitches were made, and the illustration below shows a convenient way of storing shaped
lace pieces.   The example was worked in Coats chain
mercer crochet 20 on size 2mm (14) needles.

S PIRAL E DGING

```
|CCC7CCC|||8||||/|   8
||█||||||15|||||█    7
||00|||9|||0/|█||    6
||█|||7||0//00|█     5
||00||5||0/|*||/|    4
||█||0/||6||█        3
||00|0/||5||█||      2
||0||5||/00|█        1
```

Cast on 11 stitches and knit 1 row

Row 1: Sp, K1, 02, K2tog, K5, 0, K2
Row 2: K2, 02, K1, 0, K2tog, K5, P1, K2
Row 3: Sp, K6, K2tog, 0, K3, P1, K2
Row 4: K2, 02, K5, 0, K2tog, K3, K2tog, K1
Row 5: Sp, K1, 02, (K2tog)2, 0, K7, P1, K2
Row 6: K2, 02, K9, 0, K2tog, K1, P1, K2
Row 7: Sp, K15, P1, K2
Row 8: C7, K8, K2tog, K1

Repeat rows 1 to 8

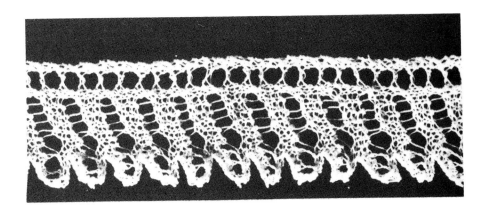

As its name implies, this edging spirals round, and is
meant to be used on deeply curved edges. You can see
from the two photos that the full effect of the pattern is
lost if the shaping isn't done properly. A good way to
arrange the shaping is shown in the illustration opposite.

This is 'real' knitted lace - that is, there are single
strands of yarn showing up in the lace. The example
shown here was knitted in Coats chain mercer crochet 40
on 1.5 mm (16) needles.

*W*HEEL *E*DGING

```
|CC6CCC||||11|||||     12
||||11|||||/0||0/▪     11
▪|▐▌|▐▌||||11|||||     10
//00/00|4||/0||0/▪      9
 ▪/||||||15|||||||      8
||||11||||/0||0/▪       7
▪|▐▌|▐▌▐▌|▐▌|||8||||     6
|/00/00/00||/0||0/▪      5
 ▪||||||14||||||        4
|||8|||/0||0/▪          3
▪|▐▌|▐▌|||8||||          2
||00/00|/0||0/▪          1
```

Cast on 12 stitches and knit 1 row

Row	1:	Sp, K2tog, 0, K2, 0, K2tog, K1, 02, K2tog, 02, K2
Row	2:	Sp, K2, P1, K2, P1, K8
Row	3:	Sp, K2tog, 0, K2, 0, K2tog, K8
Row	4:	Sp, K14
Row	5:	Sp, K2tog, 0, K2, 0, K2tog, K1, (02,K2tog)3, K1
Row	6:	Sp, (K2,P1)3, K8
Row	7:	Sp, K2tog, 0, K2, 0, K2tog, K11
Row	8:	Sp, K2tog, K15
Row	9:	Sp, K2tog, 0, K2, 0, K2tog, K4, (02, K2tog)2, K2tog
Row	10:	Sp, (K2,P1)2, K11
Row	11:	Sp, K2tog, 0, K2, 0, K2tog, K11
Row	12:	C6, K11

Repeat rows 1 to 12

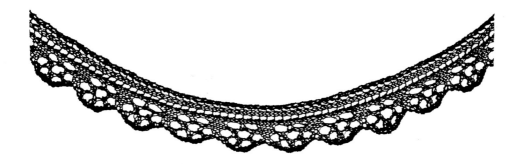

The clever placing of the double eyelets emphasises the
shaping of this edging - the almost circular shape con-
trasts well with the more jagged and pointed edges of
many of the other patterns.

As the first illustration shows, the pattern does not
produce a deep curve. However, it looks very pretty
with a ribbon threaded through the top border, and can
be gathered for an attractive ruffle, as shown below.
A light starching is best as it allows the lace to hold
its shape but to stay flexible.

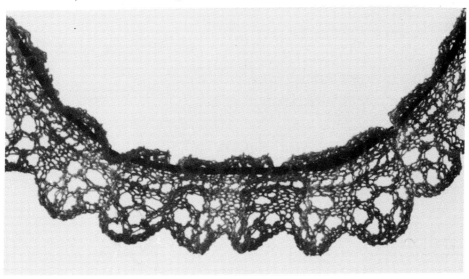

*M*ARGUERITE *B*ORDER

```
|CCC8CCCO███████9█████|0/0/|   8
|/00/00||6|||/0/0//0/0|█   7
|||█|██████████10████|0/0/|   6
|/00/00||/0||0≠0/0/0|█   5
|||█|||███████8█████|0/0/|   4
|/00/00|||0/≠0/0/0|█   3
|||█|||████████7███|0/0/|   2
|/00/00/0|||0/0/0|█   1
```

Cast on 16 stitches and purl 1 row

Row 1: Sp, K1, (0,K2tog)2, 0, K3, 0, (K2tog,02)2, K2tog, K1

Row 2: K3, P1, K2, P7, K1, (0,K2tog)2, K1

Row 3: Sp, K1, (0,K2tog)2, 0, SK2tog, K2tog, 0, K3, (02,K2tog)2, K1

Row 4: K3, P1, K2, P8, K1, (0,K2tog)2, K1

Row 5: Sp, K1, (0,K2tog)2, 0, SK2tog, 0, K2, 0, K2tog, K2, (02,K2tog)2, K1

Row 6: K3, P1, K2, P10, K1, (0,K2tog)2, K1

Row 7: Sp, K1, (0,K2tog)2, K2tog, 0, K1, 0, K2tog, K6, (02,K2tog)2, K1

Row 8: C8, P9, K1, (0,K2tog)2, K1

Repeat rows 1 to 8
Treat the two yarn overs of row 7 as separate stitches when casting off on row 8.

A reasonable knitting skill is required to make this lace.
It's shown here knitted in pearl cotton 8 on 2.5 mm (12)
needles. Though both yarn and needles are larger than
those used so far for the lace edgings, the pattern still
produces a very open, unmistakably lacy piece of knitting.

You can see from the illustration on the inside front cover,
that you can starch and shape the piece to stand on its own -
a pretty crown for a child to play with, a lining for a
bread basket or an unusual decoration for the inside of a
bowl. Used flat the edging makes a lovely collar, the
deep curve being useful for outlining a low-cut neckline.

$\mathcal{U}$NIT $\mathcal{E}$DGING

```
/ |4| |▮▮| |6| | |   16
▮▮4▮▮|/00//|0| |▬   15
/ | |5| |▮▮| |6| | |   14
▮▮5▮▮|/00//|0| |▬   13
/ | |6| | |▮▮| |6| | |   12
▮▮6▮▮|/00//|0| |▬   11
/ | | |7| |▮▮| |6| | |   10
▮▮4▮▮ |▮▮|/00//|0| |▬   9
0| |/00/| |▮▮| |6| | |   8
▮▮6▮▮|/00//|0| |▬   7
0| | |7| | |▮▮| |6| | |   6
▮▮5▮▮|/00//|0| |▬   5
0| |6| | |▮▮| |6| | |   4
▮▮4▮▮|/00//|0| |▬   3
0| |5|▮▮| |6| | |   2
▮▮▮|/00//|0| |▬   1
```

Cast on 12 stitches and knit 1 row

Row	1:	Sp, K2, 0, (K2tog)2, 02, K2tog, P3
Row	2:	0, K5, P1, K6
Row	3:	Sp, K2, 0, (K2tog)2, 02, K2tog, P4
Row	4:	0, K6, P1, K6
Row	5:	Sp, K2, 0, (K2tog)2, 02, K2tog, P5
Row	6:	0, K7, P1, K6
Row	7:	Sp, K2, 0, (K2tog)2, 02, K2tog, P6
Row	8:	0, K2, K2tog, 02, K2tog, K2, P1, K6
Row	9:	Sp, K2, 0, (K2tog)2, 02, K2tog, P2, K1, P4
Row	10:	K2tog, K7, P1, K6
Row	11:	Sp, K2, 0, (K2tog)2, 02, K2tog, P6
Row	12:	K2tog, K6, P1, K6
Row	13:	Sp, K2, 0, (K2tog)2, 02, K2tog, P5
Row	14:	K2tog, K5, P1, K6
Row	15:	Sp, K2, 0, (K2tog)2, 02, K2tog, P4
Row	16:	K2tog, K4, P1, K6

Repeat rows 1 to 16

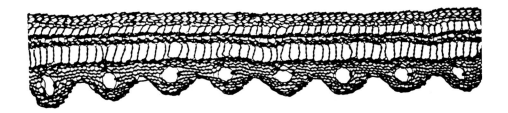

Though the instructions for this edging are rather long there is nothing intrinsically difficult about the pattern. This lace has a jersey base and needs starching to avoid the scallops turning back on themselves. It's a pretty addition to many fabrics, and is definitely straight.

The two types of faggot ladder illustrate two ways of using these to decorate the 'straight' or border side of many edgings. If you particularly like them, you can substitute them for other border patterns used in other laces. The instructions for Fern-Leaf Edging have been written up with the border given separately so that any other border can be substituted. The charts make it easy to separate the borders from the rest of the pattern.

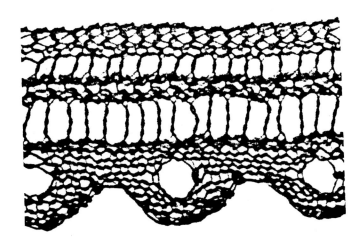

*F*LUTED *B*ORDER

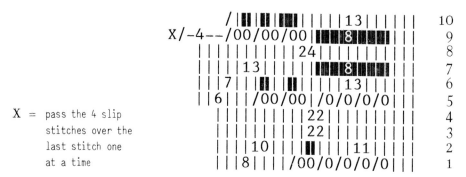

X = pass the 4 slip
stitches over the
last stitch one
at a time

Cast on 21 stitches and knit 1 row

Row 1: K3, (0,K2tog)4, 02, K2tog, K8
Row 2: K10, P1, K11
Row 3: K22
Row 4: K22
Row 5: K3, (0,K2tog)4, K1, (02,K2tog)2, K6
Row 6: K7, P1, K2, P1, K13
Row 7: K3, P8, K13
Row 8: K24
Row 9: K3, P8, K1, (02,K2tog)3, Sk4, K2tog; pass slip
       stitches over last stitch one at a time
Row 10: K2tog, K1, P1, K1, P1, K1, P2, K13

Repeat rows 1 to 10

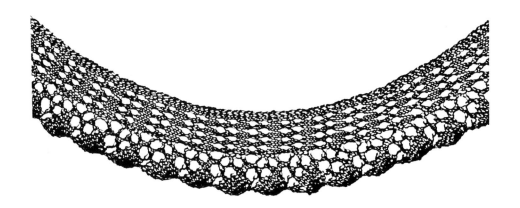

Though wider than the edgings used so far, this lace is
particularly easy to make, yet very effective. Worked
here in a fairly thick Coats mercer crochet 20 on 2.25 mm
(13) needles, the result is a gently curving lace with
two quite different sides. Choose the one you prefer.
The smooth, or jersey, side shows the 'flutes' of the
name. The gently scalloped border makes a most attractive finish for a collar and cuff set. You could extend
the width quite easily to make deeper cuffs.

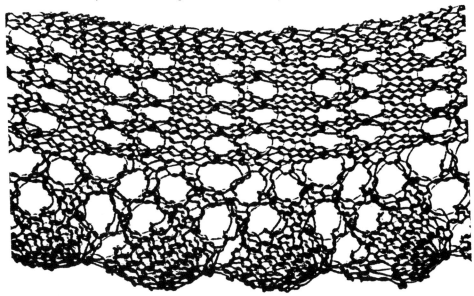

$\mathcal{P}$ARISIAN $\mathcal{E}$DGING

```
|CC5CC|█████ 9 █████0/|  12
||6|||/00/0≠0/0/0|█       11
||█|█ |||██████11█████0/| 10
||000||00/0|≠|0/0/0|█      9
 |4|███████13██████0/|     8
|||00/0||≠||0/0/0|█        7
|CC5CC|█████████15███0/|   6
||6|||/00/0|||7|||0/0/0|█  5
||█|█|||███████13████0/|   4
||000||00/0||5||0/0/0|█    3
 |4|██████11█████0/|       2
|||00/0|||0/0/0|█          1
```

Cast on 15 stitches and purl 1 row

Row 1: Sp, K2, O, (K2tog,O)2, K3, O, K2tog, O2, K3
Row 2: K4, P11, O, K2tog, K1
Row 3: Sp, K2, O, (K2tog,O)2, K5, O, K2tog, O2, K2, O3, K2
Row 4: K2, P1, K1, P1, K3, P13, O, K2tog, K1
Row 5: Sp, K2, O, (K2tog,O)2, K7, O, K2tog, O2, K2tog, K6
Row 6: C5, K2, P15, O, K2tog, K1
Row 7: Sp, K2, O, K3tog, O, K2tog, O, K2, SK2tog, K2, O,
         K3tog, O2, K3
Row 8: K4, P13, O, K2tog, K1
Row 9: Sp, K2, O, K3tog, O, K2tog, O, K1, SK2tog, K1, O
         K3tog, O2, K2, O3, K2
Row 10: K2, P1, K1, P1, K3, P11, O, K2tog, K1
Row 11: Sp, K2, O, K3tog, O, K2tog, O, SK2tog, O, K3tog,
         O2, K2tog, K6
Row 12: C5, K2, P9, O, K2tog, K1

Repeat rows 1 to 12

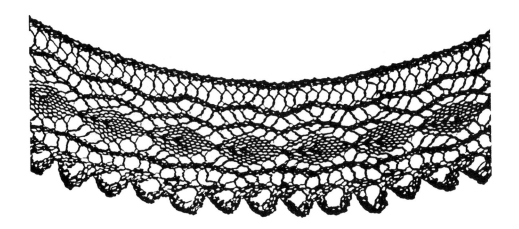

The solid oval shapes are knitted in jersey to emphasise the contrast between them and the open lace outlining them.   Though there is very little natural curve in this lace, the large triple eyelets are not displayed to their full advantage unless the lace is dressed to show them.   The two illustrations show two ways of dressing this lace.

*E*DITH *L*ACE

```
|CCC7CCC||||||16||||||||    8
|||||||||||23|||||||||||▆   7
|||||||||||24||||||||||||   6
||||10||||/0/0/0/0/0||▆     5
|||||||||||24|||||||||||    4
||X4XX|||||13||||||▆        3
|||||||||20||||||||||       2
|/c4cc/0/0/0/0/0|||▆        1
```

X = (P1,K1) into one stitch

Cast on 17 stitches and knit 1 row

Row 1: Sp, K3, (0,K2tog)5, c4, K2tog, K1
Row 2: K20
Row 3: Sp, K13, (P1,K1) into each of the next 4 stitches, K2
Row 4: K24
Row 5: Sp, K3, (0,K2tog)5, K10
Row 6: K24
Row 7: Sp, K23
Row 8: C7, K16

Repeat rows 1 to 8

Cast on 15 stitches and knit 1 row

Row 1: K2, 04, (K2tog,0)5, K2tog, K1
Row 2: K12, K1, P1, K1, P1, K2
Row 3: K18
Row 4: K18
Row 5: K2, 05, K2tog, K1, (0,K2tog)6, K1
Row 6: K15, K1, P1, K1, P1, K3
Row 7: K22
Row 8: K22
Row 9: C7, K1, 04, (K2tog,0)5, K2tog, K1

Knit rows 1 to 9
Repeat rows 2 to 9; row 1 is a foundation row

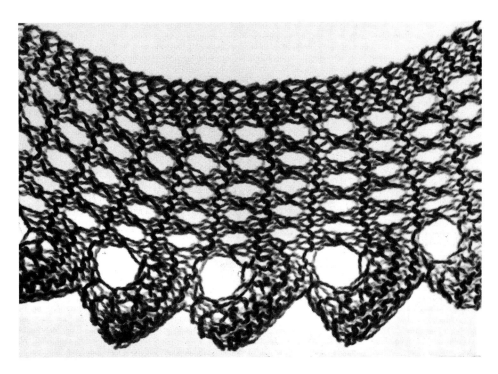

There are several versions of this lace, and two hand
knitted ones are given here. The coarser lace, made in
Lyscordet and on 2.5 mm (12) needles, makes use of 4 cast
on stitches before the end of the second row to make the
very large lace hole. The finer lace, knitted in Coats
chain mercer crochet 40 on 1.5 mm (16) needles, uses two
sets of multiple overs. These large eyelets spread out
attractively when the lace is fitted on a cylindrical
shape, and form a little skirt, as shown in the machine
knitted version illustrated on page 2. Photographed
on the flat, the lace loses some of its charm.

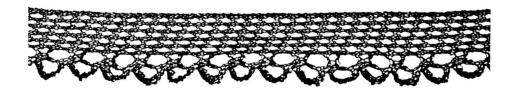

Fantail Lace

```
                              | | | |9| | | |0/0/|   12
                              X| | |7| | |/0/0█       11
                  TTTTT12TTTTT0| | |7| |0/0/|         10
                  | | | | | | |18| | | | | |/0/0█      9
                  | | | | | | |19| | | | | | |0/0/|    8
                  █|█| |█| |█| |█| |█| |█|/0/0█         7
                  /00/00/00/00/00/00|0/0/|             6
                  | | | | |12| | | | |/0/0█             5
                  | | | |13| | | | |0/0/|               4
                  █|█| |█| |█| |█|/0/0█                 3
                  /00/00/00/00|0/0/|                    2
                  | | |8| | | |/0/0█                    1
```

T = 3 throws

X = Slip next 12 sts to
    RHN, dropping loops,
    Now slip them to
    LHN and knit them
    all off as 1 st.

Cast on 14 stitches and knit 1 row

Row   1:   Sp, K1, (0,K2tog)2, K8
Row   2:   (K2tog,02)4, K1, (0,K2tog)2, K1
Row   3:   Sp, K1, (0,K2tog)2, K1, (P1,K2)3, P1, K1
Row   4:   K13, (0,K2tog)2, K1
Row   5:   Sp, K1, (0,K2tog)2, K12
Row   6:   (K2tog,02)6, K1, (0,K2tog)2, K1
Row   7:   Sp, K1, (0,K2tog)2, K1, (P1,K2)5, P1, K1
Row   8:   K19, (0,K2tog)2, K1
Row   9:   Sp, K1, (0,K2tog)2, K18
Row 10:   (T3)12, 0, K7, (0,K2tog)2, K1
Row 11:   Sp, K1, (0,K2tog)2, K7; slip next 12 stitches
               to RHN dropping extra loops, then slip all 12
               back to LHN and knit them off as one stitch
Row 12:   K9, (0,K2tog)2, K1

Repeat rows 1 to 12

A number of traditional lace edgings use elongated stitches
to make a pretty and unusual finish.   I have given my own
adaptation of this lace.   The little 'fans' at the lower
edge will puff outwards if you don't flatten them, giving
a more than usually 3-D effect.   This is a gently curving
lace, very pretty for edging semi-circular shawls.   It is
worked here in Twilleys 20s crochet yarn on 2 mm (14) needles.

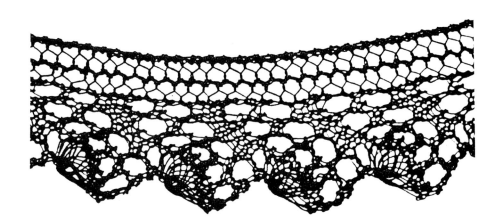

Pierrepoint Edging

```
|CC5CC||5||0/|||0/|0/|   8
||||10|||0/|||0/|4||■    7
||■||5||0/|||0/|||0/|    6
//00|||/0|||/0||7|||■    5
||■||■||/0|||/0|4||0/|   4
|00/00||/0|||/0||5||■    3
||■|||/0|||/0||0/|       2
||00||5||0/|||0/||■      1
```

Cast on 17 stitches and knit 1 row

Row 1: Sp, K2, K2tog, O, K3, K2tog, O, K5, O2, K2
Row 2: K3, P1, K3, K2tog, O, K3, K2tog, O, K2, O, K2tog, K1
Row 3: Sp, K5, O, K2tog, K3, O, K2tog, K2, O2, K2tog, O2, K2
Row 4: K3, P1, K2, P1, K1, K2tog, O, K3, K2tog, O, K4, O,
         K2tog, K1
Row 5: Sp, K7, O, K2tog, K3, O, K2tog, K3, O2, (K2tog)2
Row 6: K3, P1, K5, O, K2tog, K3, O, K2tog, K3, O, K2tog, K1
Row 7: Sp, K4, K2tog, O, K3, K2tog, O, K10
Row 8: C5, K5, O, K2tog, K3, O, K2tog, K1, O, K2tog, K1

Repeat rows 1 to 8

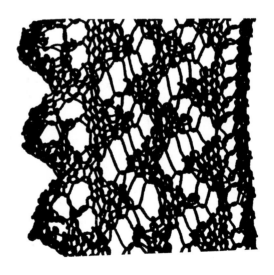

This very pretty lace uses knitting in its true lace form,
and single yarn strands decorate the zigzag shapes.   The
enlargement opposite shows precisely how the single yarn
strands lie and the chart clearly outlines the zigzags and
shows how they are made.   However, the illustration of a
longer piece gives a much better overall impression of the
charming effect of this lace edging.

The enlarged version, illustrated below, of the Spider
Edging given on page 19, again shows how very effective
single strands of yarn can be for knitted lace.

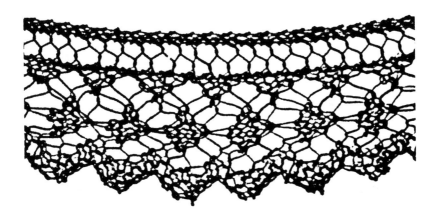

|C4CC||0█|██|X*|4|| 8
||0/0||X*/█+█*+0|▬ 7
||6||█X█|██████|4|| 6
||0/0|||0/0|0+0|▬ 5
||5||0|██|█X*|4|| 4
||0||X*/█+█*+0|▬ 3
|4||█X█|██████|4|| 2
||0|||0/0|0+0|▬ 1

█ = (K1,P1)3 in one
stitch

X = C5 of X, leaving 1
stitch

Cast on 13 stitches and knit 1 row

Row 1: Sp, K1, 0, SKtog, 0, K1, 0, SK2tog, 0, K3, 0, K2

Row 2: K4, (K1,P1,K1,P1,K1,P1)all in next stitch, P2, K1, P3, K4

Row 3: Sp, K1, 0, SKtog, (K1,P1,K1,P1,K1,P1)all in next stitch, SKtog, P1, K2tog, C5, K2, 0, K2

Row 4: K5, 0, K1, P1, K1, P1, C5, K4

Row 5: Sp, K1, 0, SKtog, 0, K1, 0, SK2tog, 0, K3, 0, K2tog, 0, K2

Row 6: K6, (K1,P1,K1,P1,K1,P1) all in next stitch, P2, K1, P3, K4

Row 7: Sp, K1, 0, SKtog, (K1,P1,K1,P1,K1,P1) all in next stitch, SKtog, P1, K2tog, C5, K2, 0, K2tog, 0, K2

Row 8: C4, K2, 0, P1, K1, P1, K1, C5, K4

Repeat rows 1 to 8

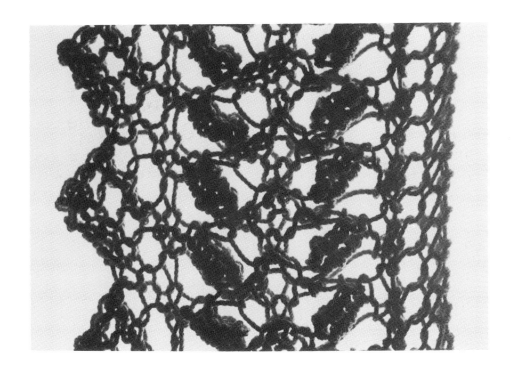

This very unusual and beautiful knitted lace is made by
knitting 6 times into a single stitch on one row and
casting off 5 of these stitches on the next.   This produces a chunky texture and this, combined with the lace
holes, adds a further dimension to the lace.   In fact,
if it was not for the lower border, one would be hard put
to say this was a knitted lace.

Worked in a fine silver or gold yarn, this pattern looks
sensational over dark velvet.   Knitted here in Coats
chain mercer crochet 10 on 2 mm (14) needles.

FERN-LEAF EDGING

```
|CCC7CCC|||||12|||||█||||█|||     16
|||||||||18|||||||/00//00/|█      15
||█|||||||16||||||█||||█|||       14
|/00||X|||11||||||/00//00/|█      13
|4|█|||||14|||||█||||█|||         12
||/00||X|||9|||||/00//00/|█       11
||5|█||||12|||||█||||█|||         10
|||/00||X||7||||/00//00/|█         9
||6||█||||10|||||█||||█|||         8
|4||/00||X||5||/00//00/|█          7
|||7|||█||8|||█||||█|||            6
||5||/00||X|||/00//00/|█           5
|||8||||█||6|||█||||█|||           4
||6|||/00||X|/00//00/|█            3
||||9|||█|4|█||||█|||              2
|||7|||/00||/00//00/|█             1
```

X = c4 sts on LHN
    K these 4 sts, then:
    using LHN lift st 3
    over st 4, st 2 over
    st 3 and st 1 over
    st 2. 1 st left.

Cast on 21 stitches and knit 1 row

Row 1: Sp, K1, K2tog, 02, (K2tog)2, 02, K2tog, K1 = B
         K1, 02, K2tog, K7
Row 2: K9, P1, K1
         K3, P1, K3, P1, K3 = B'
Row 3: B, X, K2, 02, K2tog, K6
Row 4: K8, P1, K3, B'
Row 5: B, K2, X, K2, 02, K2tog, K5
Row 6: K7, P1, K5, B'
Row 7: B, K4, X, K2, 02, K2tog, K4
Row 8: K6, P1, K7, B'
Row 9: B, K6, X, K2, 02, K2tog, K3
Row 10: K5, P1, K9, B'
Row 11: B, K8, X, K2, 02, K2tog, K2
Row 12: K4, P1, K11, B'
Row 13: B, K10, X, K2, 02, K2tog, K1
Row 14: K3, P1, K13, B'
Row 15: B, K17
Row 16: C7, K9, B'

Repeat rows 1 to 16.

44

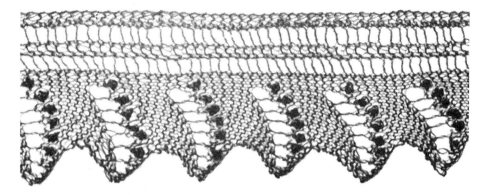

Texture can be added to knitted fabric in various ways.
Here a simple technique is used to emphasize the outline
of the lace and to give the edging a different character
from the laces shown so far.   Knitted here in pearl
cotton 5 on 2.5 mm (12) needles. The enlargement of one
complete pattern shows the texture in detail.

The fairly wide repeating border is given separately so
that other borders can be substituted in the pattern. It
can easily be isolated on the chart by drawing a vertical
line between the 11th and 12th columns from the right
hand side

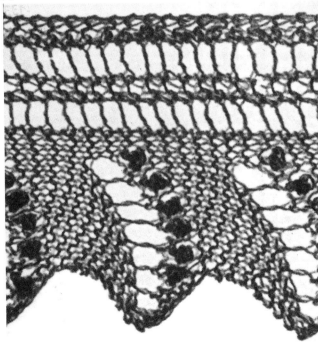

45

Machine Knitted Laces

A number of quite well-known traditional laces can be transposed
for machine knitting. The patterns given here are not the only
interpretation of these traditional patterns; you will soon find
that you can work out your own version. However, they do give
pleasing results, and were chosen to illustrate a number of ways
of producing edgings reasonably quickly on the machine.

A certain amount of handwork is necessary for most of these
edgings in order to get interesting shapes in the form of scallops,
or shells, or points of various kinds; only one lace is truly
automatic. However, it is still possible to produce these laces
very much faster than the hand knitted ones. When edging large
fabric pieces, this obviously matters.

The lace edgings illustrated here demonstrate the use of a particular
modern machine to work patterns characteristic of similar hand
knitted patterns. You can adapt others and enjoy creating your own
new laces. These will be just as genuinely creative as if you had
used knitting needles. Machine knitting is a relatively new craft –
automatic transfer lace machine knitting is a very new one, and
it is up to you, the contemporary knitter, to produce patterns
that future knitters will be as glad as you to use.

I used the Knitmaster 260 KL machine. All punchcards should be
inserted in the machine with the right hand side of the illustration
used as the bottom edge. I have assumed an adequate cast on in
waste yarn and the correct adjustment of the autotension.

INCREASES AND DECREASES

The simple machine increase made by pushing an extra needle out
to the B or working position makes a picot edge. In order to have
a picot on the decrease part of the pattern, lift 2 stitches onto
the two adjacent working needles, then bring the empty needle next to
them to the B or working position, and push the other back to the A
or non-working position.

*S*YMBOLS AND *A*BBREVIATIONS

RC   = row counter

RHS   = right hand side

LHS   = left hand side

sts   = stitches

0   = centre of needlebed

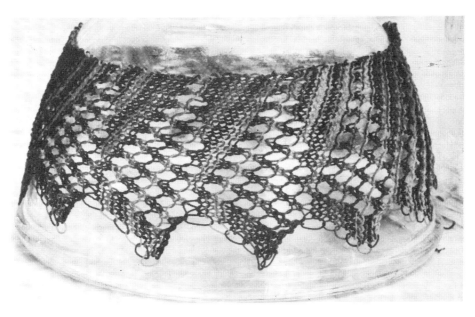

This machine knitted edging, worked here in a random dyed crochet cotton, can easily be shaped on an upturned pudding bowl.

ƷIG ƷAG

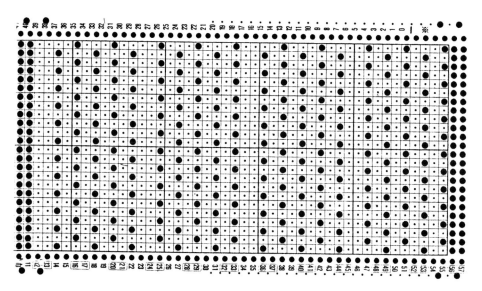

Carriage at right or left, set card on row 1   RC

Cast on the number of stitches wanted, setting them
symmetrically on either side of 0.
Set edge pins at both edges

Knit 2 rows
Release card and set machine for lace knitting   0
Knit for length wanted; each section has 11 rows   11 etc.

Repeat rows 1 to 11

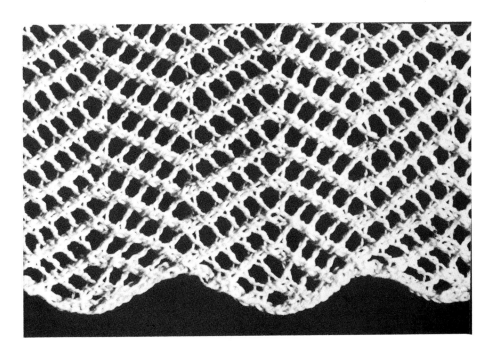

This completely automatic zigzag is the ideal beginner's
lace. The number of stitches cast on depends on the width
of edging wanted; the yarn can be quite thick to very fine,
the carriage can be on the right or on the left to start the
lace.

The natural bias of the faggotting will push the edges into
points or soft undulations, depending on how the edging is
dressed. Anyone can make this lace, and it is attractive
enough to be used for many purposes. Make it in any yarn,
to any width, for any length. Finish on a multiple of 11
to get even ends. Worked here in Lyscordet on tension 8.

49

GODMOTHER LACE

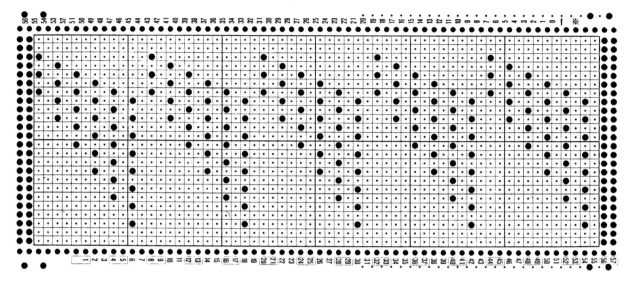

Carriage at right, set card on row 1   RC

Cast on over 12 stitches to the Left of 0
        8 stitches to the Right of 0

Knit 2 rows   0
Release the card and set machine for lace knitting
Increase 1 stitch on the RHS of the next row and knit   1
Knit 1 row   2

Repeat this 4 times   10

Cast off 5 stitches at the beginning of the next row   11
Knit 1 row   12

Repeat these 12 rows

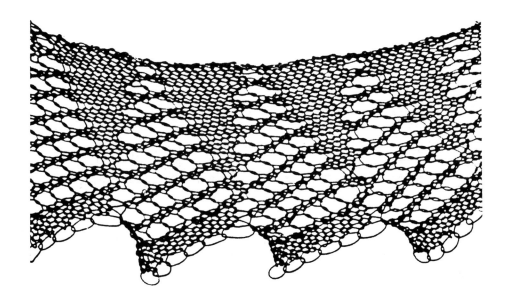

A simple little lace, much favoured by godmothers in Vic-
torian times for edging their godchild's christening robes.
The machine version is just as pretty, and it's quick to
make - appropriate for modern godmothers.

Because there are five increase rows on the right hand side
this edge is longer than the left hand edge and, properly
dressed, the lace has just enough curve to be useful for a
curved hemline or an edging for a circular shawl.   The
inherent bias also helps to increase the shaping.

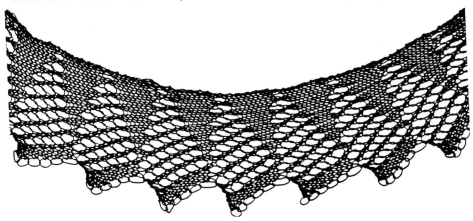

*C*OCKLE *S*HELL

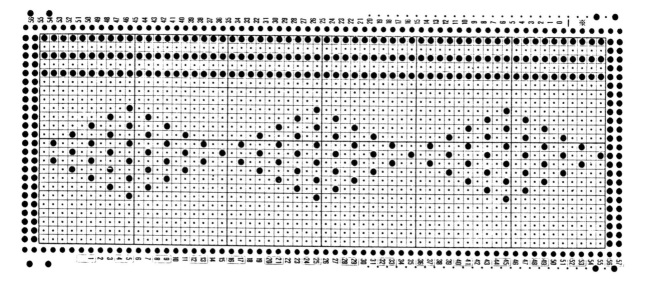

Carriage on the right, set card on row 1   RC

Cast on over 5 stitches on the Left of 0
               14 stitches on the Right of 0
Knit 1 row
Release card and set machine for lace knitting   0
Increase one stitch on LHS on next and every following
alternate row 5 times   9
Knit 1 row   10
Decrease 1 stitch on LHS on next and every following
alternate row 5 times by putting two stitches to their
adjacent needles to the right, putting one of the
empty needles to A position and leaving the adjacent
empty needle in B position   19
Knit 1 row   20

Repeat rows 1 to 20

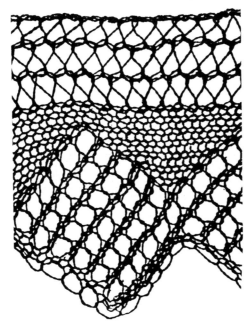

This very well-known traditional pattern takes many forms; here the simplest faggot diamond is used, producing an almost square shape due to the bias of the constant decreases in the same direction.

The edging can easily be worked by starting with the carriage at the left, changing the direction of the bias. This is how the enlarged illustration was worked. It is easier for left-handed knitters, whose needs are often ignored. The right-handed version, made with the card inserted so that the faggoting is on the left, is knitted here in a 20s crochet cotton on tension 4.

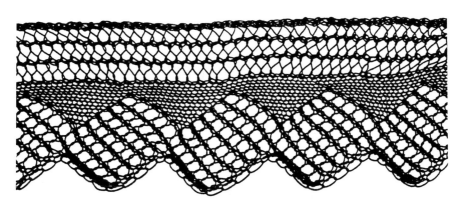

$\mathcal{V}$AN $\mathcal{D}$YKE $\mathcal{B}$ORDER

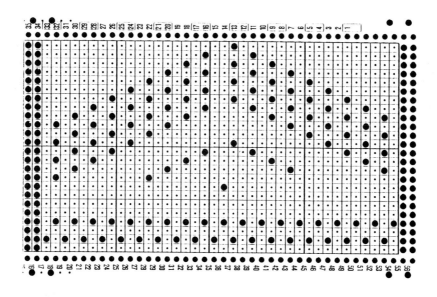

Carriage at right, set card on row 1   RC

Cast on over 12 stitches on the Left of 0
          6 stitches on the Right of 0
Set red knob between stitches 14 and 15 on RHS
Knit 2 rows
Release card and set machine for lace knitting   0

Knit 2 rows   2
Increase 1 stitch on RHS on next and every alternate
row 9 times   19
Knit 1 row   20
Take the double transfer tool, put 2 stitches from
the RHS on the next two stitches nearer 0, push one
needle back to A and keep the empty needle nearer
0 at B
Knit 2 rows   22
Repeat these 2 rows 8 times   38

Repeat rows 1 to 38

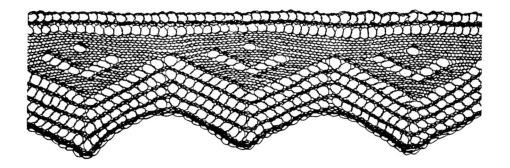

The 'Van Dyke' formation is a commonly recurring theme in much lace knitting. In this version, a quadruple border, punched along the lines of a zigzag lace, is reinforced by a smaller repeat pattern. The contrast of the completely straight faggot edging accentuates the lace points.

Though the pattern itself would tend to make the lace go to a point, these are much emphasised by increasing and decreasing with the pattern, making deep points prettily outlined in picot stitches. This is a quick and easy lace to knit, shown here in a fairly heavy 3s cotton knitted on tension 5.2.

OPEN SHELL

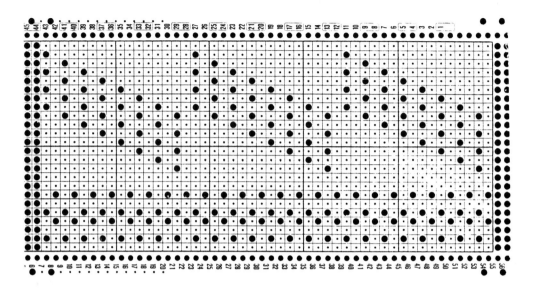

Carriage at right, set card on row 5   RC

Cast on over 12 stitches on the Left of 0
                7 stitches on the Right of 0
Set edge pin at LHS and between stitches 13 and 14
on RHS

Knit 2 rows
Release card and set machine for lace knitting   0
Increase 1 stitch on the RHS of the next and
every alternate row 7 times   13
Knit 1 row   14
Put stitches 8 to 14 on the RHS on a transfer tool
and place them all on stitch 7 on the RHS of 0
Push needles 8 to 14 back to A
Knit 2 rows   16

Repeat rows 1 to 16

This dainty, open lace, is easily worked on the machine in
a 40s crochet cotton and tension 3.1.   Though there are
seven increases, the decrease is worked on one stitch only -
that is seven stitches are all decreased to a single stitch,
so that the extra length produced by the increases is bent
into an attractive curve, or shell, at the lower edge of
the lace.

The double faggot lace at the upper edge is in keeping with
the open nature of this lace.   The result is straight,
so that this is a suitable lace for edging pillow cases,
rectangular tablecloths, napkins, handkerchiefs...

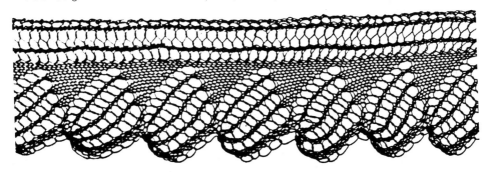

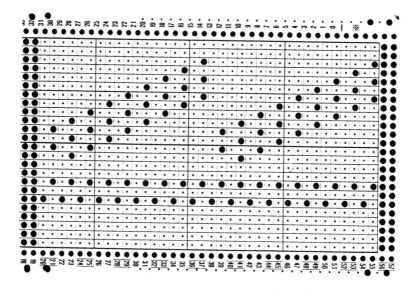

Carriage at right, set card on row 1   RC

Cast on over 9 stitches on the Left of 0
                13 stitches on the Right of 0

Knit 2 rows
Release card and set machine for lace knitting   0
Knit 4 rows   4
Increase 1 stitch on the RHS of the next and every
following 4th row 3 times   13
Knit 4 rows   17
Take the treble transfer tool, lift the 3 RHS
stitches and place them over the next 3 stitches
on the right of 0
Push the empty needles back to A
Knit 1 row   18
Repeat rows 1 - 18

Carriage at right, set card on row 1
Knit 3 rows before releasing card   0

58

Knit 3 rows   3

Increase 1 stitch on the RHS of the next and every
following 4th row 3 times   12

Knit 4 rows   16

Decrease 3 stitches as given for carriage at right
and knit 2 rows   18

Repeat rows 1 to 18

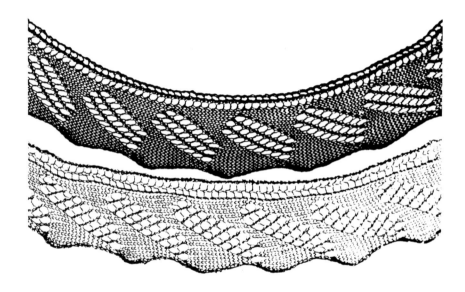

Two versions of this lace are shown in the photograph; the
first, made with the carriage starting at the right, is
knitted in a 20s crochet on tension 4.1. The second, made
with the carriage started at the left, is knitted in the
finest crochet cotton available, DMC 120, on tension 2.2.

The three increased stitches are decreased in a relatively
unusual way - all three are taken and put over THREE of the
original stitches; a quick but quite different finish for
the right hand side.

$\mathcal{C}$LARENCE $\mathcal{B}$ORDER

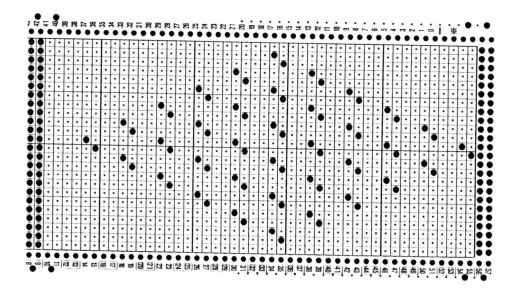

Row Pattern Repeat:
Knit 2 rows with the machine set to select and transfer
WITHOUT YARN followed by 2 rows with the machine set to
knit WITH YARN up to row 44 (RC reads 22); knit 2 rows.

Carriage at right, set card on row 1

	Rows	RC
Cast on over 14 stitches on the Left of 0		
9 stitches on the Right of 0		
Set an edge pin at LHS		
Knit 2 rows		
Release card and set machine for lace knitting		0
Knit 6 rows	6	2
Increase 1 stitch on the RHS on the next and every		
following 4th row 4 times	19	9
Knit 7 rows	26	12
Decrease 1 stitch on the RHS on the next and every		

	Rows	RC
following 4th row 4 times by putting 2 stitches on their adjacent needles to the left, putting one of the empty needles to A position and leaving the one nearest 0 in the B position	39	19
Knit 5 rows	44	22
Lift the strand of yarn lying under needle 1 on RHS of 0 over that needle		
Knit 2 rows	46	24

Repeat rows 1 to 46 (RC 1 to 24)

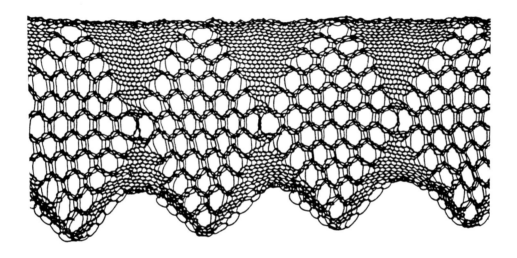

Completely automatic machine knitted double eyelets are easy to design provided the 'staggered' or 'drop' formation is used for the basic pattern. However, the edging given here needs one manual lifting of a yarn bar to make it look very similar to its hand knitted version.

$\mathscr{M}$ACHINE $\mathscr{E}$DITH $\mathscr{L}$ACE

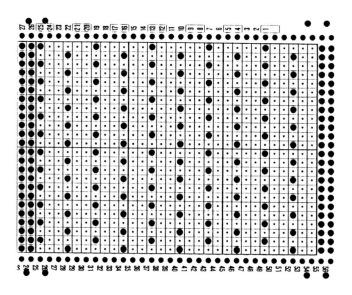

Carriage on the right, set card on row 1   RC

Cast on over 14 stitches on the Left of 0
           17 stitches on the Right of 0
Set an edge pin at LHS
Knit 2 rows
Release card and set machine for lace knitting   0
Knit 1 row   1
Take the double transfer tool and move the last 2
stitches on the RHS to needles 18 and 19, and
transfer stitch 15 to needle 14. Knit 2 rows   3
Lift the yarn bar under needle 16 over that needle
Knit 1 row   4
Take the double transfer tool and put stitches on
needles 18 and 19 on needles 16 and 17
Push needles 18 and 19 to A position
Knit 2 rows   6

Repeat rows 1 to 6

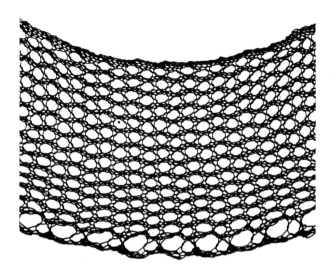

The illustration above shows the lace worked to the pattern
given, using a 20s crochet cotton on tension 4. The second
version is made in the same way but with an edge pin at the
RHS between needles 16 and 17, worked in a 3s cotton on tension
5.2.   The edging can easily be made wider or narrower by
adjusting the number of needles in use to the left of 0.

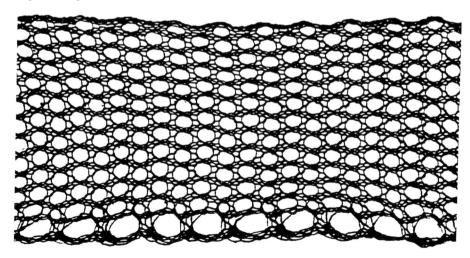

SUPPLIERS

Fine knitted laces are best worked in fine yarns of good quality. Handknitters will also need fine needles. The following are sources of both yarns and needles **at the time of going to press.** Please note that these items may go out of production at any time, owing to small demand from the public. PLEASE SEND A STAMPED, SELF-ADDRESSED ENVELOPE for current availability and prices if you wish to buy any of the items listed below.

FINE YARN AND THREAD MANUFACTURERS

Please send an SAE for information on your nearest stockist to:

J & P Coats (UK) PLC, Anchor Mills, Paisley, PA1 1JW

DMC, C & F Handicrafts, 346 Stag Lane, Kingsbury, London, NW9

Twilley Ltd, Roman Mills, Stamford, Lincs PE9 18G

A mail order service for Coats, Twilley and DMC yarns is at present available from Broiderwise, on Glastonbury (0458) 32533.

KNITTING AIDS

Please send a **stamped, self-addressed envelope** for a price list and description of knitting aids, including steel knitting needles.

6.75 inch length 15s and 16s fine steel knitting needles, **while stocks last**	The Thorn Press, The Old Vicarage, Dept A, Godney, Wells, Somerset BA5 1RX
16 inch length, 16s and thicker steel knitting needles	Anderson & Co, Shetland Warehouse, Lerwick, Shetland, ZE1 0BD
16 inch length, 16s and thicker steel knitting needles	Stove & Smith, 98 Commercial St, Lerwick, Shetland